# Redshift

# Redshift

Bernd Sauermann

Text: Copyright © Bernd Sauermann 2015

Cover Imgage: Copyright © Shin-Yeon Moon 2015

All rights reserved

ISBN: 978-1-943170-06-7

Cover Art: Shin-Yeon Moon
Cover Design: Jane L. Carman
Interior Design: Alyssa Hanchar
Production Director: Jane L. Carman
Typfaces: Cambria and Gothic Ultra

Published by: Lit Fest Press, Carman, 688 Knox Road 900 North, Gilson, Illinois 61436

There are no rules.
festivalwriter.org

# Acknowledgements

Many thanks to the editors of the following publications where some versions of the following poems have, or will have, appeared:

> *Anti-*
> *Right Hand Pointing*
> *Luna Luna*
> *Kansas Quarterly Review of Literature*
> *Poems Underwater*
> *Open 24 Hours*
> *Cultural Weekly*
> *Mad Hat Review*
> *The Round Table*
> *Nice Marmot*
> *Posit*
> *The Enchanting Verses Literary Review*
> *Cease Cows*

*for my mom and dad*

# Table of Contents

| | |
|---|---|
| In the Beginning | 15 |
| Tidal | 16 |
| Ferrous | 17 |
| Some Similes | 18 |
| Conversation | 19 |
| Dress Up | 20 |
| Skeleton Key | 21 |
| Blue Flame | 22 |
| The Silence Mill | 23 |
| Bird Song | 24 |
| The Hands | 25 |
| Negotiation | 26 |
| Resurrection | 27 |
| Occurrence | 28 |
| A Prophecy | 29 |
| Pastoral | 30 |
| Keyhole | 31 |
| The Scent of Dark | 32 |
| The Wet Season | 33 |
| Revelation | 34 |
| Tropic of Cancer | 35 |
| The History of Texas | 36 |
| Fairy Tale | 37 |
| Slow Dance | 38 |
| Tonight's News | 39 |
| Happy Birthday | 40 |
| Momentary | 41 |
| Event Horizon | 42 |

| | |
|---|---|
| Lye | 43 |
| Hindsight | 44 |
| Snapshot | 45 |
| Confessional | 46 |
| Desiccant | 47 |
| Leaving Town on Halloween | 48 |
| Recognition | 49 |
| Pushing On | 50 |
| The Artist | 51 |
| Pallor | 52 |
| Killing Day | 53 |
| Past Tense | 54 |
| Astronomy | 55 |
| The Weather | 56 |
| Dream Hand | 57 |
| A Gift | 58 |
| Purchase | 59 |
| Redshift | 60 |
| Hocus Pocus | 61 |
| In the Garden | 62 |
| The Sure Sign | 63 |
| Language | 64 |
| Small Numbers | 65 |
| The Wind in the Oleander | 66 |
| New World | 67 |
| Obsolescence | 68 |
| Recessional | 69 |
| Portents | 70 |
| The Passage of Time | 71 |

# In the Beginning

She whispers lies to a clock and a wedding ring shines like a new appliance while he falls to his knees and begs. A child is born in a lamp-lit room. Another child has vanished like a fear. All of these things are true when a blue dust settles like decades of bad headlines. Pages torn daily from a paperback Bible gather in a drawer. There is a locked door in the silence of the cellar, and there is so much power in what a man says that a boy can see what isn't there. All boys can see what isn't there, but no woman can make a clock stop reciting its feverish prayer.

# Tidal

A father laughs nervously when a door closes like a woman's hand and rage obscures the view from the attic window. There is a man sweeping the street. A car passes in the rain and hisses a promise which fades like the Milky Way at sunrise. A shell is pressed to an ear. Almost daily, pictures curl at the edges like incoming waves.

# Ferrous

An old man's voice rumbles down a cobblestone street as the smell of diesel is married to the sharp slap of memory. A bus pulls away from a curb. A cloud of exhaust suggests long-lost generations of steel, and locomotives and buses bring the old man to his knees at the altar of a moment. There is the sound of a hammer on an anvil. There are the ghosts of boxcars moaning in the station. There was a time the old man believed in the power of steel, but then a national anthem was sung in a dead child's voice.

## Some Similes

A word breaks the morning like a dropped glass of water. An old man stumbles in the street. Years later, a joyous recollection braces like the scent of snow in the courtyard or the odor of diesel in the rain. Already, a red boot has been sucked deep into the mud, and as a clock tower topples, the old man drops to the sidewalk like the king of hearts discarded in favor of a black queen. A stacked deck of cards burns like hardwood in the stove.

# Conversation

Time thrusts its shadows onto a woman in the next room who speaks in jagged tones to someone else. Someone has died. Someone has always died. The clock ticks viciously on the wall, and the heart of the woman is also not quiet. The same goes for every other person. Of course, none of this matters to me. None of this means anything to anyone, and those hours were, these decades later, anyone's time for the taking.

# Dress Up

An old toy train circles my heart as a switch is thrown and the room sizzles with electricity. The scent of orange rind rises from the wood stove as layers of memory are peeled back with a knife, but truly, I see that a cup overflows with years. I see an old woman badgered by the fear of sharp objects in a drawer. I enter an attic full of the trappings of a recent war. Slowly, I unpack them, make them mine, and then I fight forever the wars of an old man. In an old man's attic, I put on forgotten clothes and howl like a doomed train.

# Skeleton Key

There are teeth under the bed where a boy sleeps. A door opens and a mother figure walks in. The boy falls in love with a secret, and the secret falls in love with a skeleton key. A lock appears and opens itself like memory. Sometimes, it's almost too much to bear.

# Blue Flame

If a sentence or a phrase causes friction, it is because someone's words are taut like oiled leather. A blue-green stain surfaces like a bruise while land speed records are shattered at Bonneville. A rocking boat makes a little boy cry because he hasn't yet learned to speak the language of water. Bluer and bluer, colder and faster, the syntax of water pulls him under.

# The Silence Mill

The stench of the steel mill is cracking his teeth while an old man doesn't move too far or too fast but works silently on a crossword for mutes. Black elbows pass for self-discipline. Then the old man searches for a word he's forgotten like a man searches for a word of a language he's never known. In another room, in another sentence, the subject is understood.

# Bird Song

A pair of hands in the bushes flutters like a bird, and a girl's skin smells warm in the afternoon. With her hands tucked under her head, she feigns sleep. Her face is flushed. I show her my hands and tell her to think of them as birds. She cries and I hold her weeping hands and comfort her. Years later, I learn that feathers drift to the ground like a handful of notes of a song about a vague memory of the cinnamon scent of skin.

# The Hands

In the branches of a fig tree, some children practice making hand shapes, then invent new games: Hammer down the Manhole, Smother like a Dog, A Cat in the Grass, A Bird in the Window, Dirt Clods. Later the children again pay attention to their hands. They attend to a formation of throwing hands. They attend to secret handshakes, and they attend to an army of incandescent, brightly glowing hands. I tell you this because I have warm hands.

# Negotiation

Sometimes an olive tree is more than just a tree. I say this as if I know what I'm talking about. The truth is I know nothing, except that there is a bird in the oleander and I'd rather sit cross-legged in a field of dry grass than run a race for the love of a girl who will give me up for a few burning words. I hold her hand hostage in an olive tree while another hand signals anxiously as the ransom is being negotiated.

# Resurrection

Years have passed since anyone has last seen the old woman hobble up the hill to church for Easter. The congregation commemorates this by hiding colored eggs in the high grass where the children will not find them until the following year. They pray so hard. They pray so hard for deliverance. They pray so hard that someone is risen.

# Occurrence

The sound of our voices dissipates like the thin mist of that morning a million small lives were lost in vapor. We were surrounded by the ghosts of dead things, dead limbs, dead trees. A trip to the hospital solved nothing. Or so October's nurse told us. A faint beeping could be heard. Then it stopped. All this to say autumn was in our midst, winter looming in our immediate future.

# A Prophecy

A plane hurtles me into the future where dirty water from a garden hose will not slake my thirst. A blue bike passes on the road. A prophecy is thus fulfilled and a frequent flyer is my one true friend. The farmer's daughter whispers invitations through an open window while two women comb each other's hair at the fence. I deny a spider entrance to a keyhole as a name fades more slowly than contrails in an anxious sky. Somewhere in the house a key turns in a lock.

# Pastoral

The children are asleep in the fields and more silent than flowers. I tell you this in a tiny voice, my words closer together than the spaces between the beats of a hummingbird's heart. Is a once fertile phrase now heavy with vines and ivy? Is my ear filled with severed leaves? Are blades of grass just now snapping at the wind? I knew it would come to this. I knew it would come to this blue day with clouds moving quickly off, out over the pasture.

# Keyhole

An unspoken plea is still alive, but the key in the lock has been removed. A towel hangs wet and sad, forgotten in a cold shower. A spider finds itself alone on a vast white wall. These are the lies told to no one but myself: An arm is warm at night. We barely touched each other. You remember, don't you? The silent weight of your head on my arm? The brush of legs? The light of day through a blinding keyhole?

# The Scent of Dark

Hope hinges on a bead of sweat as we come to a new understanding of fear on the bluff. Large animals haunt our small talk, and the beautiful fish in the bucket are dropped and left for dead. A cinderblock wall offers protection. Later we lay cupped in the moist palm of the night and I pretended to be your American friend. My ears tremble to the sound of your breathing. Your hair smells warm and your mouth tastes foreign. The coolness of your skin in the damp dark startles me. Something smolders, too, off somewhere in the night.

# The Wet Season

During typhoons, conventional wisdom holds that a window should always be opened on the downwind side of the house, but then we went out during the eye of the storm. In the hours to come, we will walk along cinderblock walls between houses as a native girl teaches us traditional ways of addressing the rain. Then a sudden downpour announces itself like a stone thrown on a dark tin roof. We jump into the dark. How did we come to be so wet? How did we come to be so far from home? Whose dream is this?

# Revelation

We put dead things in boxes and bury them in the sand, and we put our wet hands on a defective fan. We hold things underwater. All of these to test our mettle, but later, all the news would be bad—the curfew had been broken, the typhoon was on its way, the revolution had begun, and the prophecy would be fulfilled, night after night like a recurring nightmare, like day after day of steaming rain. This was the curse. This was the revelation making its way like mad current up my arm.

# Tropic of Cancer

Pleasure hides itself in the monsoons, in the shadows of palm and papaya, the jackfruit, the trembling stillness of the Tropic of Cancer. Like a warm snake, desire crawls the length of my legs. Spiders the size of my hands are everywhere, and as a keyhole turns around me like jungle, something in my chest burns like a heart.

# The History of Texas

Throughout history, a woman has kept a man's heart in her locket, and her dance was performed for specific reasons known only to her. Throughout history, messages have been sent and received over sweltering wires. Even now, the pony express. Even now, remember the Alamo.

# Fairy Tale

The party is over and a girl walks home, a story folded neatly in her shoe. It's a fairy tale in which a shoe box holding some pressed flowers is hidden under a bed like a priceless treasure. At some point in the story, boys gather and point to a cardboard cutout of a slipper that's much too small. The step-aunt is a given. It's like this on page after page after page.

# Slow Dance

When? When will he learn that a slow dance with the shy girl passes like a silent year in the dark? When will failure not whisper from the pauses between minutes shuffling like his feet? When will these shoes not creak like the door to an era closing?

# Tonight's News

While dancing on a doghouse in the rain. While taunting the neighbor with a little loud music. While trading weeping love for a kiss behind the dark garage. It's like the movie in which I run headlong into the woods while the jukebox plays "One of These Nights" over and over. In a parallel universe, another girl is imaginary, and in related news, a man blows a kiss at gravity from the top of a tall tower.

# Happy Birthday

A birthday wish like the sharp swish of an ax. An ax handle. A flood uncoiling suddenly like a snake. I light candle after candle as she blows them gently out, teasing the wind with hot syllables that ooze like sweat from my every pore. I tell the neighbors I am three words on a birthday girl's tongue. Don't read this. Don't tread on me.

# Momentary

Someone asks for a light in a language of her own invention. I want to stay, I say, but must make my way to the station. It's clear that at least one language has remained unlearned. And it's clear that at least one cellar door is kept locked for a reason. With his hand on a key in his pocket, a boy searches for the word for "fire," but then the moment is lost in a perfect rendition of what can only be described as a moment.

# Event Horizon

This calendar has no heart. The years have no pulse, and weeks are silent as gravity. On what day did we lean in to kiss under a nonchalant sun? What month is orange and yellow? What vow is blue? I thought I knew but all that remain are sad and calculated seasons spiraling slowly toward an event horizon.

# Lye

There are vows like ink of the letters of words of a poem printed on the pages of a burned book, its ashes long since made into soap. Forever. Always. Never. I beg her to repeat these words until they are scrubbed of all meaning.

# Hindsight

The night passes like a headache. War and death are imminent. Could we have guessed a dark basement where there are bars on the window? Looming bicycles? Stacks of empty luggage in the corner? Could we have guessed a life raft hundreds of miles from the sea? Years later, these memories rolling back and forth like dead things in the surf?

# Snapshot

She tells me a photo of the sky is always more memorable with one cloud in it. Right now, someone else dreams of a camera pointed toward the slight chance of rain. Right now, someone else is in love with the distant possibility of birds. Right now, this has been recorded.

# Confessional

A divine decade to mull over. Full of sorrow and full of black precision and grace, he carves his disappointments on the head of a pin. Motionless, like ten broken fingers, ten angels weep hymns in attendance, then sit listening intently like ten years of silence in a dark cathedral.

# Desiccant

Back in the desert a vow is broken under an impossibly blue sky. Every day for a week I drive past the cemetery of hope. Every day for a week I dig a new hole. Every day for a week I learn a new word for "stick" and see that promises tumble like heartbroken weeds. And every day for a week another wall falls revealing a dried-out vow, seven dead words withered in the heat.

# Leaving Town on Halloween

The words driven from between my teeth: listen, remain at a constant speed, set the clock, clock the miles, one by one, and proceed in any one direction till an ocean gets in your way. The only answer is a questionable destination and an obsession leads me to believe in one one-thousandth of a picture: where a fear grows on a vine and matures as a pumpkin rolling down a hill on Halloween, young girls cry like swerving cars on Main St. Do not believe anything else.

# Recognition

School lets out and a white shirt is retired like an obsolete persona. Walking in a borrowed face, I see an old friend across the street. I greet him and he tells me a woman has brought him to town. I give him a gift made of woven hair. "Keep this," I say to him, "so you'll remember whose face is written in the stars."

# Pushing On

A late snow settles like a sigh as a wind circles the extinct volcano. When we get back into town, there is a car crash and we drive a woman to the hospital. Later, she comes back to us and cries and I leave again, this time for good. Even later, the snow is falling again. It falls heavily on my eyes as I push on toward the pass.

# The Artist

All the rain that's ever fallen hangs in the air between us as she starts to paint the sky. The leaves are beginning to cut the thin light of another dismal morning. I think, "Not gray again," but when I suggest to her to start over, she says the day has been spoken for by clouds. Her brush flits back and forth on the canvas, and the leaves, the leaves start to hiss, my God, how they start to dance.

# Pallor

"Wolf howl on snow crust air," she says, as if memory is not to be trusted. All the while murmuring her gray song. All the while her hands feeling in vain for the sky. All the while a pallor settling like the gray aroma of old coffee in a dim late-night diner. Coffee after coffee. Cigarette after cigarette. Sky after numb sky. Somehow, I have to get out of this.

# Killing Day

Remembered: the night before, the sound of desperate crying snaking its way through the outlet from the adjacent room. A story fabricated on request, repeated again and again and again until it was true. Then driving toward a cauldron of steaming, filthy water, cold light setting on the frozen lake like a receding syllable. Noticing, only then, the knife in my hands. All this, on some level, peaceful.

# Past Tense

A book on figure drawing plagues me like a dry kiss. Surely, I can break my standoff with a phrase that sticks in my throat like a horrible scratch. Surely, a mouth. Surely, a hand held and one last time. Surely, those days without end, the books, the paintings. Surely they were.

# Astronomy

The Northern Lights fail to signal an end approaching. Down at the lake, an omen drops into the cold water as a pair of unfamiliar hands makes the sign for *forest*. A silent gesture circumscribes a notion. Something ominous exists far beyond the faint line of trees, beyond the distant lights in the village. Dogs bark as a satellite arcs toward the horizon. The tolling of the meetinghouse bell attends midnight. Our stars plunge to their death one after another.

# The Weather

Right now it rains outside in urgent whispers of promise and we speak in low tones about the weather. "Sooner or later it'll let up," you offer. I answer, "It's really black now but I think I see some stars over there." You say, "This weather will change for the better," and I suggest, "The calm before the storm." Almost in unison we say, "I wish it would stop," and then you add, "The sky's too tight," and that's why the silver fields of our faces are tarnishing toward midnight.

# Dream Hand

Gently entering the town in his dream, bodily controlling the turns of his sleep, the new woman plays it like a trump card, laying it down on his burning chest. It's the sun coming up on the highway. It's better than even odds. It's the sparkle of Vegas, and it's a game to walk in on, holding the winning hand in light of the doomed moon.

# A Gift

A gift is given out of season. A candle flickers and then goes out. Someone, another woman, turns comfortably in sleep as I gaze at the starless ceiling. I mouth some words while the woman makes gestures as if handing over something small and fragile.

# Purchase

For a few minutes, a book distracts him from everything. The sun shining. A river happily playing itself through the rocks. But then next door, a woman rants at length about a man, then sobs breathlessly. Except for the woman's crying, it's an idyllic scene. So he turns to the next chapter. He reads a few more lines, a few more pages. The story seems familiar. A sale follows. The price goes without saying.

# Redshift

Mid-sentence, her demeanor changes. He should have known, should have seen it coming, the stem of the glass snapping like a thin bone in a hand. Another hand closing like a heavy-handed rhyme. The rhyme giving in to stone, and the stone slowly ground to sand in an hourglass. All this in the minutes before dawn. All this in the moments to come.

# Hocus Pocus

A slim chance shimmers like a liquor store at dusk. An incantation issues from my mouth: "All across Europe as the new day arrives, there are the old ways to remember. Here the hills are new, yellow and red and green and blue; here we find gold in the hills, then drive south past the satellite dishes. How do you improve on the car with the most non-stops to Europe? Edsel. Dresden. Right down to my goddamn roots. Right down to my goddamn roots." What follows is a clumsy gesture, the wave of a sad, misshapen hand, wild wishes clinking like bottles.

# In the Garden

A woman strolls in the perennial garden. The moon flowers, datura inoxia, are in full bloom. What would a poisonous flower trade for a phrase whispered at midnight? And why this fluttering of hands like the wings of a mute swan?

# The Sure Sign

I cover the miserable miles to the kitchen to trash myself among the sheets of your last letter in which you tell me you have died. With a steady hand, I write back telling you that, though I am not dead, I am now invisible. I write this with an unseen finger in the thick dust which has been gathering on the table since we shared a meal made from our last two potatoes. Just then everything becomes very clear: they were our last two potatoes.

# Language

One word is white and written in the dust and another word is black and written in the snow. Some boot prints track away from my window through which an early sun shoulders its way. This is not an attempt at prayer, as if faith is anything more than a stalled front, as if no man ever slept on the floor amidst laundry. I've told you this before in a language you can't understand; I lie awake at night praying for the color green.

# Small Numbers

The new year barely under way and already I'm sick of rain and telephones. In silent stretches of swaying wire our words pass each other like flicks of light, while the distance looms, dark, drawn out, and an electric hum connects stiff pauses to meaning. Words coil like cable in the silence, twisted from repeated motions, the constant hanging up, twisted from you insisting we are small numbers listed in a thick book. The cord stretches. The numbers add up.

# The Wind in the Oleander

There's more to life than kites and string and a bottle of wine, and there's more to life than a bottle of wine and the wind. You are dreaming, she says, of oleander. Yes, it's the oleander, I tell her. It's always the oleander, she says, but who will sing from the bushes on this warm and fragrant evening while a kite flies tied to a windmill? I am the kite, I tell her, and you are the glistening tether.

# New World

I learn the French word for "swallow." I say hello to rum and bourbon and say good morning to a new pair of hands, first in one language and then another. I say hello to a new dance as the sun kisses a day of weather breaking like a heatwave. Another sun fades in the rear-view. Hello again white teeth, my blazing days, your smile in a mouth of new construction.

# Obsolescence

No longer a stick tossed into the torrent and no longer a slow walk down a long black hall. No longer one tasteless pint downed after another in front of some flickering TV. No surreptitious phrase in the corridor of a cringing mouth, no freezing footprints in the snow of a collapsed day, and no longer a scent lingering like hours spent in a room filled with rusting knives.

# Recessional

I float on the warmth of her fingers through my warm hair. Our future hangs in the trees like Spanish moss, and the bayou rises to meet the laughter of a woman. Later, a contract is drawn up: I will gather moss, and a laughing girl will watch the rain wet my hair. She'll describe to me the rain in glances, and I'll take in rich syllables, someone who used to blister in the dry heat, a red sun receding in the cracked rear-view mirror, an angry history rolling off like a burning car into the sunset.

# Portents

The weather breaks as I smoke a Camel on returning from Texas. I confess: I have eaten meat this evening, and my giddiness circles the moon tracing an orbit which has no beginning and no end. A star dives headlong into the shimmering lake. The black water burns with iridescent fish. So we are told.

# The Passage of Time

Down by the lake certainty shifts to ponder the moment. Is this really the way it works? A blink and it's ten thousand years later and the sole connection between us is electronic, like a synapse, like a nerve impulse? Small words contemplate their meanings. A vague memory of water comes to mind, surfaces like a bobbing apple. Other apples rot in a ditch. Is any of this to be believed? Can this minute be trusted to define a phrase muttered what feels like only a moment ago? Is this hello or good-bye?

www.ingramcontent.com/pod-product-compliance
Lightning Source LLC
Chambersburg PA
CBHW071240090426
42736CB00014B/3165